ROCKS AND MINERALS

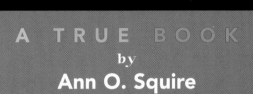

A TRUE BOOK

by
Ann O. Squire

Children's Press®
A Division of Scholastic Inc.

New York Toronto London Auckland Sydney
Mexico City New Delhi Hong Kong
Danbury, Connecticut

Capital Reef
National Park

*Reading and
Content Consultant*
Jan Jenner

*Author's Dedication
For Evan*

*The photograph on the cover
shows a rocky coastline.
The photograph on the title
page shows igneous rocks.*

Library of Congress Cataloging-in-Publication Data

Squire, Ann.
     Rocks and minerals / by Ann O. Squire.
          p.   cm. – (True Books)
     Includes index.
     Summary: Introduces different types of rocks and minerals and where
they are found.
          ISBN 0-516-22505-7 (lib. bdg.)   0-516-26985-2 (pbk.)
     1. Rocks—Juvenile literature. 2. Minerals—Juvenile literature.
[1. Rocks. 2. Minerals] I. Title. II Series: True book.
QE432.2 S65 2001
552—dc21   2001005759

Contents

This kitchen counter
is made of granite.

Rocks All Around Us

You probably don't think much about rocks, and even less about minerals. But did you know that some of the most familiar things in your world are made of rocks? The sidewalk and the roads outside your house, the sand at the beach, maybe even the counters in

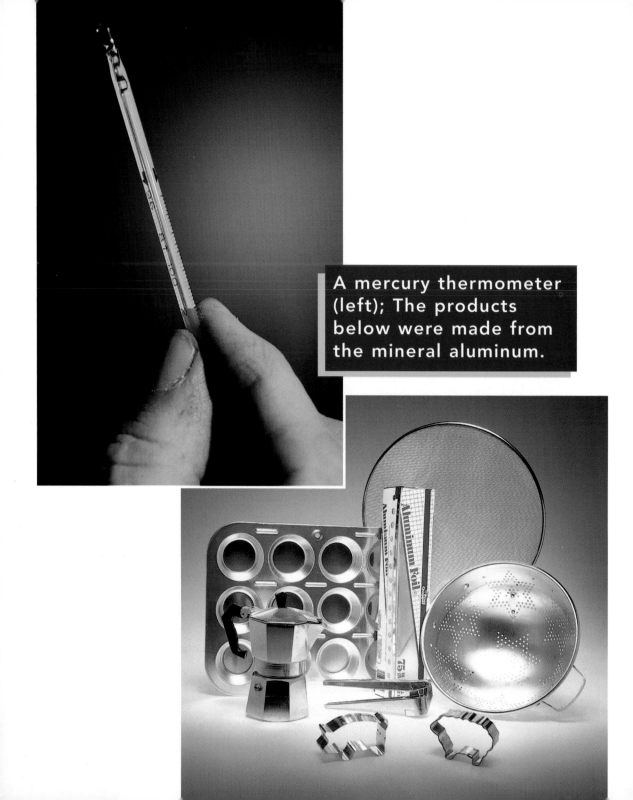

A mercury thermometer
(left); The products
below were made from
the mineral aluminum.

your kitchen or the floors in your bathroom—all of these are made of rocks. Minerals are even more common. Without minerals, we wouldn't have batteries, coins, magnets, tin cans, mercury thermometers, or aluminum foil.

"OK," you might be saying. "Rocks and minerals are all over the place. But what do they have to do with each other?"

Many houses and sidewalks are made from different kinds of rocks.

The answer is simple. Minerals are the building blocks from which rocks are made. And rocks and minerals together are the building blocks not just of sidewalks and roads, but of the very Earth we live on. Our Earth is, in fact, a gigantic ball of rock that measures nearly 8,000 miles (12,875 kilometers) across and weighs about 6.6 sextillion tons (6.7 sextillion metric tons).

Earth's outer skin (the part we live on) is called the crust. The crust is made of rock, and is about 45 miles (72.4 km) thick at its thickest point. The crust beneath the oceans is

thinnest. Here it may be only about 3 to 5 miles (4.8 to 8 km) thick. Scientists have tried to drill through the crust to explore the deeper layers, but so far they haven't been successful.

Beneath the crust is the mantle, a thick layer of very hot rock. In some places, the rocks are so hot that they actually melt, forming a soft, syrupy material called magma.

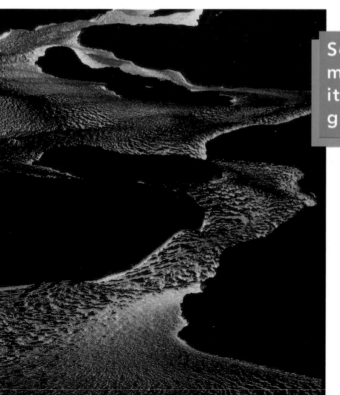

Sometimes magma forces its way above ground.

Sometimes the hot magma forces its way up through cracks in Earth's crust. As we'll see later, this is one of the ways that rocks are formed.

Underneath the mantle is Earth's outer core—a hot, dense liquid made of the minerals nickel, iron, and perhaps sulfur. At the very center of Earth is the inner core, which is a heavy, dense, solid ball made of nickel and iron.

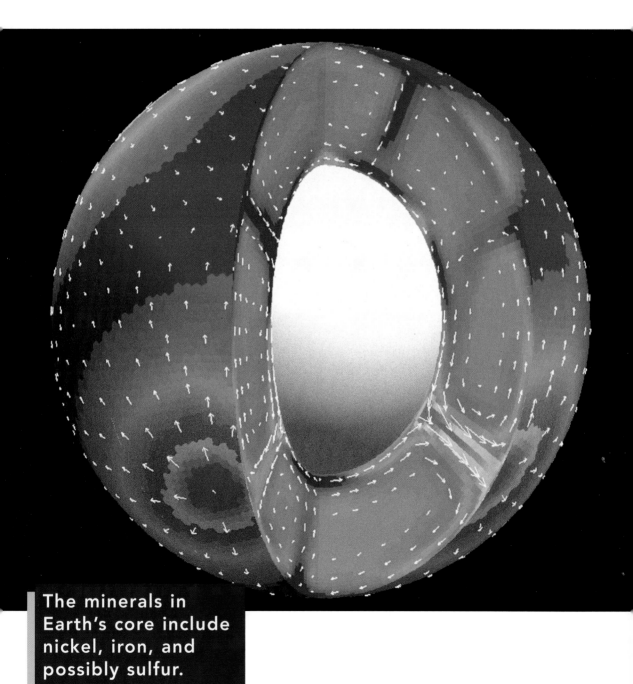

The minerals in
Earth's core include
nickel, iron, and
possibly sulfur.

What Are Minerals?

Now you know that rocks are made of minerals. But what exactly are minerals? They are inorganic (not living), solid substances that are made up of basic chemical elements such as oxygen and calcium. Minerals occur naturally—that is,

A ruby is
a mineral.

they are not created by
people. Minerals are found
everywhere in our lives, even
in the food we eat. Spinach

The salt we put on our food is the mineral halite.

and sunflower seeds are rich in the mineral iron. Nuts contain the minerals copper, zinc, and manganese. Common table salt is actually a mineral called halite. Your

The minerals manganese, copper, and zinc are found in nuts.

toothpaste probably contains the mineral fluorite to help prevent cavities. Metals such as lead, silver, and gold are

Sometimes minerals, such as this ruby, take the form of crystals.

minerals. So are gems such as diamonds, rubies, and emeralds.

Many minerals take the form of crystals. They can look like diamonds, cubes, or other regular geometric shapes. In some rocks, such as granite, it is possible to see the tiny mineral crystals that make up the rock.

Besides having their own special shapes, minerals also have different colors, different weights, and different degrees of hardness. Talc, which is used in making dusting powder, is

Talc is the softest mineral on the Mohs scale.

Sometimes people put talc powder on their hands so they can have a firm grip on something.

the softest of all minerals. It rates only "1" on the hardness scale that ranges from 1 to 10. The scale was developed in 1812 by a mineralogist named Friedrich Mohs. A diamond, the world's

hardest mineral, rates "10." Every mineral has a place somewhere along this scale. Corundum, the mineral that makes up rubies and sapphires, is very hard, rating "9" on the Mohs scale. Graphite, the mineral used in making pencil leads, is very soft, rating only between "1" and "2."

How Are Rocks Formed?

Now that you know a bit about minerals, let's see how they come together to create rocks. There are three types of rocks in the world, each formed in a different way. One of the most common is igneous rock. In fact, most of

Natural stone columns in Yellowstone National Park

Earth's crust is made of igneous rock. Igneous means "made by heat." All igneous rocks get their start in the hot magma deep within Earth.

While you read this page, pools of red-hot magma are pushing upward against Earth's crust. Sometimes the magma finds a crack in the crust and flows into it. The magma does not break through to the surface, but because the temperature near the surface

Granite is formed by slow cooling underground magma.

is lower, the magma cools and turns into rock. Granite is a very common igneous rock that is formed by the slow cooling of underground magma.

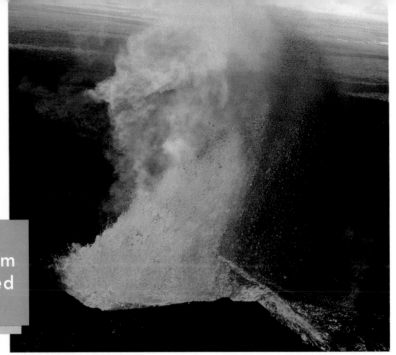

Magma that explodes from Earth is called lava.

At other times the hot magma actually escapes through a hole in Earth's crust in a volcanic explosion. The escaping magma is called lava. Lava cools much more quickly than magma trapped underground, so it forms different kinds of igneous

When lava cools very quickly it forms obsidian (left). Pumice (below) is formed from lava that has many gas bubbles.

rocks. Obsidian is a shiny black glass that is created when lava cools very quickly. Pumice is a light, spongelike rock that is formed from frothy lava. Gas bubbles in the lava give the pumice its hole-filled appearance.

Sedimentary rock has many different horizontal layers.

The second kind of rock is called sedimentary, and it is formed in a completely different way from igneous rock. Powerful natural forces such as wind, heat, cold, and the movement of glaciers are responsible for the first step. These elements wear away mountains and grind up rocks into tiny pieces. Rain and rivers wash away the pieces (called sediments), until they settle on the bottom of lakes and seas.

As more and more layers of sediment build up, the pressure from the upper layers turns the deeper layers into rock. Sandstone and limestone are two types of sedimentary rock. If you look closely at sedimentary rocks, you can often see different-colored layers in them. These layers come from different mineral sediments that built up over many years. Sedimentary rocks are also the place to find fossils of

This Colorado plateau has been worn away by erosion.

The layers of sedimentary rock are different colors because they contain different minerals.

prehistoric plants and animals. These delicate fossils are never found in igneous or metamorphic rock because they would be destroyed by the high heat and intense pressure.

The third type of rock is called metamorphic (which means "changed"). Every metamorphic rock started out as either a sedimentary or an igneous rock. Heat and pressure are the two forces that

This quartzite was formed when molten magma heated up sandstone.

work, either separately or together, to change a rock into a metamorphic rock. When molten magma pushes up into Earth's crust, the heat can be so great that it "bakes" all the

rocks nearby. This is the way that sandstone, a soft sedimentary rock, turns into a much harder rock called quartzite. It is also how soft limestone turns into hard, beautiful marble.

Pressure from the shifting earth changes shale to slate.

Pressure is another force
that can change rocks. When
mountains are formed, Earth's

crust bends and folds. This puts such powerful pressure on the rocks below that it often changes them from one type of rock to another. This is the way that shale, a sedimentary rock, turns into slate, a hard rock that is sometimes used to cover the roofs of buildings. Pressure is also responsible for turning granite, a hard igneous rock, into another kind of rock called gneiss.

Rocks Through the Ages

Rocks have been important to people for longer than you can even imagine. Prehistoric humans first used rocks to make tools hundreds of thousands of years ago. Among the first stone tools were axes, which were probably used for cutting wood and skinning animals.

American Indians used sharpened rocks for arrowheads.

Later on, stone was formed into sickles (for harvesting crops), as well as into daggers and arrowheads. In ancient Rome, powdered chalk and lead were used to whiten the skin, and red ocher (ground clay) was popular for coloring the lips and cheeks. Later on, people ground up rocks to make dyes and paints.

Even now, rocks are important in our everyday lives. Granite, limestone, and marble are still used in buildings. Did you know that the Empire State Building is made mostly of granite and sandstone? Cement is made from ground limestone, and bricks, pottery, tiles, and

Granite and sandstone were used to build the Empire State Building.

The Hopi Indians use clay to make beautiful pottery.

many other things we use every day are made from clay. Grinding stones are still used to grind wheat and other grains into flour. Even the chalk your teacher uses on the blackboard is a kind of rock!

Rocks From Space

Barringer Meteor Crater in Arizona

Canyon Diablo Meteorite

Iron meteorite from Russia

Meteorites are rocks that fall from space. About 20,000 years ago a huge meteorite crashed to Earth in what is now Arizona, leaving a hole 3/4 of a mile (1.2 km) wide and 600 feet (182.9 meters) deep. After the meteorite exploded, it left about 30 tons (30.5 metric tons) of rock fragments scattered all over the countryside.

To Find Out More

Here are some additional resources to help you learn more about rocks and minerals:

 **Books**

Blobaum, Cindy. **Geology Rocks!: 50 Hands-On Activities to Explore the Earth.** Williamson Publications, 1999.

Burton, Jane. **The Nature and Science of Rocks.** Gareth Stevens, 1998.

Challoner, Jack. **Investigations: Rocks and Minerals.** Lorenz Books, 2000.

Kittinger, Jo S. **A Look at Minerals: From Galena to Gold.** Franklin Watts, 1998.

Tejada, Susan. **Dig It! How to Collect Rocks and Minerals.** Reader's Digest, 2001.

Organizations and Online Sites

Children's Museum of Indianapolis
www.childrensmuseum.org/ geomysteries

The website of the Children's Museum of Indianapolis has lots of interesting information on rocks, minerals, and fossils.

Geology
kidscience.about.com/cs/ geology

Links to information about soil, caves, fossils, rocks, and minerals.

Mineral and Gemstone Kingdom
www.minerals.net

Indepth information on every known mineral.

Rocks and Minerals
ww.surfnetkids.com/ rocks.htm

Use these articles and games to learn more about the earth.

Important Words

crystal a solid mineral with a geometric shape, straight edges, and smooth faces. All crystals are made up of atoms that are arranged in a regular, orderly way.

igneous rock a rock that has been formed from cooling magma

magma molten rock found in Earth's mantle layer

metamorphic rock a rock that is formed by the action of heat, pressure, or both, on another type of rock. All metamorphic rocks are "changed" rocks.

mineral a naturally occurring substance with a definite chemical composition. Minerals usually take the form of crystals.

sedimentary rock rock that is made up of layers of sand, mud, or other sediments that have built up over many years.

Index

Meet the Author

Ann O. Squire has a Ph.D. in animal behavior. Before becoming a writer, she studied African electric fish, rats, and other animals. Dr. Squire has written many books on animals, animal behavior, and other natural science topics. Her most recent books for Children's Press include *Animals of the Sea and Shore*, *African Animals*, *Animal Babies*, and *Animal Homes*. She lives with her children, Emma and Evan, in Bedford, New York.